ideals
VALENTINE

My valentine wish
Is nothing new . . .
Each day I wish
The best for you.

My valentine's a
Daily prayer
That God will keep you
In his care

And grant your every
Dream come true . . .
This is my valentine wish
For you!

Kay Hoffman

Publisher, Patricia A. Pingry
Editor, Peggy Schaefer
Art Director, Lyman Black, Jr.
Production Manager, Jan Johnson
Permissions, Kathleen Gilbert
Copy Editor, Joan Anderson

Front and back cover by Al Riccio

Inside front cover by Gerald Koser

Inside back cover from The Photo Source

ISBN 0-8249-1059-1

IDEALS—Vol. 45, No. 1 February MCMLXXXVIII IDEALS (ISSN 0019-137X) is published eight times a year,
February, March, May, June, August, September, November, December
by IDEALS PUBLISHING CORPORATION, Nelson Place at Elm Hill Pike, Nashville, Tenn. 37214
Second class postage paid at Nashville, Tennessee, and additional mailing offices.
Copyright © MCMLXXXVIII by IDEALS PUBLISHING CORPORATION.
POSTMASTER: Send address changes to Ideals, Post Office Box 148000, Nashville, Tenn. 37214-8000
All rights reserved. Title IDEALS registered U.S. Patent Office.
Published simultaneously in Canada.

SINGLE ISSUE—$3.95
ONE-YEAR SUBSCRIPTION—eight consecutive issues as published—$17.95
TWO-YEAR SUBSCRIPTION—sixteen consecutive issues as published—$31.95
Outside U.S.A., add $4.00 per subscription year for postage and handling.

The cover and entire contents of IDEALS are fully protected by copyright and must
not be reproduced in any manner whatsoever. Printed and bound in U.S.A.

P9-DXQ-801

A February Snow

Garnett Ann Schultz

The sun shone through a snowy sky
And drifts were mounting white and high;
Just yesterday it all began—
A wondrous February Plan:
God sent white flakes, all soft and dear
To surely thrill and bless us here.

It lasted far into the night,
A beautiful and charming sight—
Each branch and tree, a rich design,
A forming bit of wintertime,
With fields and hills and country lanes
All bright and sparkling once again.

Then as the dawn rose in the east,
The sun broke through, the snow had ceased—
A world of pleasant sweet surprise,
A fairyland before our eyes.
All nature smiled, the world did glow—
God sent a February snow.

Photo Opposite
COLCHESTER, CONNECTICUT
Fred M. Dole Productions

The Bird Feeder

Ellen Van Gunst

It's time to feed our feathered friends;
Snow covers the ground once more.
So we have put our feeder out
With plenty of food in store.

The birds are wary for awhile;
They hesitate nearby.
But soon they sense that all is well,
And their hunger bids them try.

The friendly chickadee stops by,
A small, but trusting bird;
The nuthatch comes along to share—
Then leaves to spread the word.

Ere long we have a varied group
Who are our guests each day;
The flashy cardinal, with his mate,
Decides there's food our way.

A flock of sparrows comes to call—
How soon the feed is gone!
A new supply we must bring out
Before the day is done.

The saucy blue jays, not afraid,
Will come to get their fill;
The feeder must be filled again
Before another meal.

We're glad to feed our feathered friends
When winter comes our way,
And we enjoy their visiting
Our feeder day by day.

Photo Opposite
CLARK'S NUTCRACKER
Thomas Kitchin
Tom Stack and Associates

February

Edna Jaques

The fields are bedded down with snow,
    Like blankets tucked about their ears,
As if the world had gone to sleep;
    But now and then a bush appears,
Wearing a crown of purest gems
    With scarlet berries on white stems.

The windbreak running to the lake
    Has snowy trunks like silver birch;
Even the weeds have hoods of snow,
    Like quaint old women in a church;
The hens have frosted beards and look
    Like old men in a picture book.

Along the highway muffled wheels
    Go by without a breath of sound;
The fence posts stand like sentinels,
    Wearing tall helmets diamond-crowned;
The mailman in his battered truck
    Has drifted snow and ice to buck.

And yet I know that spring is nigh
    Although the wind is cold and raw,
The sky is softer than it was;
    The fields have started in to thaw,
Putting aside their winter dress
    To don their springtime loveliness.

Photo Opposite
LOWER TWIN LAKE
SIERRA, NEVADA
Ed Cooper Enterprises

February Fudge

Golden Fudge

2½ cups (1 pound) firmly packed brown
    sugar
1 cup sugar
½ cup butter *or* margarine
1 cup non-dairy liquid coffee cream
2¼ cups butterscotch wafers *or* chopped
    butterscotch blocks
4½ cups marshmallow creme
1 cup chopped pecans *or* other nuts
½ cup raisins
½ teaspoon vanilla
1 teaspoon butter-rum flavoring

Combine sugars, butter, and coffee cream in a heavy 2½-quart saucepan. Place on medium heat and stir until butter is melted. Cook without stirring to 238°, about 15 minutes. Remove from heat; add butterscotch and marshmallow. Stir until thoroughly blended. Add nuts, raisins, and flavorings. Pour into two buttered 8-inch square pans. Let set several hours until firm. Cut into squares. Keep in closed container. Makes about 8 dozen pieces.

Butterscotch Nut Fudge

¼ cup butter
1 cup brown sugar
1 cup sugar
¾ cup sour cream
1 teaspoon vanilla
½ cup chopped walnuts
    Walnut halves

Melt butter in a heavy saucepan. Add brown sugar and heat to boiling. Add sugar and sour cream. Cook over medium heat until sugar dissolves, then slightly higher heat to 236°. Without stirring, cool at room temperature to lukewarm. Beat until mixture holds its shape and loses its gloss. Quickly add vanilla and nuts. Spread immediately in a buttered 8-inch square pan. Cool and cut into squares. Garnish with walnut halves. Makes about 4 dozen pieces.

Coffee Fudge

3 cups sugar
¾ cup milk
2 tablespoons instant coffee powder
½ cup non-dairy liquid coffee cream
1 tablespoon light corn syrup
2 tablespoons butter
1 teaspoon vanilla
1½ cups (6 ounces) chopped chocolate coating *or* wafers
¼ cup finely chopped nuts

Combine sugar, milk, instant coffee, coffee cream, and syrup in a 3-quart saucepan. Cover and bring to a boil. Uncover and cook without stirring to 236°. Remove from heat; add butter and vanilla without stirring. Cool to lukewarm. Beat until candy begins to thicken; pour into a buttered 8-inch square pan. Melt the chocolate coating over hot, not boiling, water in a double boiler. Spread evenly over fudge; sprinkle nuts over chocolate. Cut into squares before candy becomes firm. Makes about 4 dozen pieces.

White Chocolate Cream Fudge

3 cups sugar
1 cup evaporated milk
⅜ cup butter
2 cups marshmallow creme
12 ounces white chocolate, cut in small pieces
1 cup chopped pecans
1 4-ounce jar candied cherries (optional)

Bring sugar, milk, and butter to a boil over low heat, stirring constantly. Cook to 237°. Remove from heat; add marshmallow creme, white chocolate, nuts, and cherries. Stir until marshmallow creme and chocolate are melted. Pour into a 13 x 9-inch buttered pan. Cool before cutting. Makes about 6 dozen pieces.

Photo Opposite
FEBRUARY FUDGE
from *Nice & Easy Desserts Cookbook*,
copyright © 1978 by Cyndee Kannenberg.
Published by Ideals Publishing Corporation,
Nashville, Tennessee.

Flowers in Winter

Elsie Natalie Brady

In frozen beds where flowers sleep
The winter snow lays soft and deep;
But here, within my cozy room,
A pot of violets are in bloom.

And pink begonias by the score
Enhance the calm interior;
The cactus, not to be outdone,
Has blossomed in the winter sun.

Yards of ivy frame the scene,
An emerald necklace for a queen,
While glowing on the windowsill,
A touch of spring. . .
         a daffodil.

Photo Opposite
WINTER GREENHOUSE
H. Armstrong Roberts, Inc.

Photo Overleaf
MORRISTOWN, NEW JERSEY
Gene Ahrens

Valentine's Day
in the Countryside

Earle J. Grant

For Valentine's Day in the countryside
Fences wear a fragile lace,
For sometime during the night snow fell
And made our farm a magic place.

A cardinal sweeps down from icy eaves,
His presence like a crimson heart,
And perches on the windowsill
(I dare not move lest he depart).

At the edge of the woodland, galax leaves
Peep from snow-encrusted sod:
Nature's valentines thoughtfully sent
From a kind and generous God.

Here comes the school bus, the children rush in,
Each one holding a valentine;
Each genuine gift of "I love you"
Wonderfully warms this heart of mine!

Photo Opposite
BROWNSVILLE, VERMONT
Gene Ahrens

What Is a Valentine?

Nadine Brothers Lybarger

A valentine is many things. . .
A token of sweet love,
A gracious way to tell someone
The things you're dreaming of.

It is a sentiment expressed
In serious mood or gay
To lover, relative, or friend
Those things you'd like to say.

It is a messenger that spans
The barrier of space
And makes a distant loved one feel
As near as face-to-face.

What, really, is a valentine?
No words will quite suffice,
Except to say it's many things
And all of them are nice.

Photo Opposite
OLD-TIME VALENTINE
The Photo Source

An American Valentine

Pamela Kennedy

I watched my parents exchange valentines and smiled with them over the sentiments expressed. One showed busy husbands parading comically around a bemused wife and opened to reveal a fold-out red heart. The other was on delicate parchment graced with pastel roses and a lovely scripted message. The cards were just a formality, really, another recognition of the love they've shared for almost fifty years. It is not a grand romance on the scale of Scarlett and Rhett's or even the Brownings, but it is a love story, honest and true, a reflection of their America, a chronicle of their times.

They were raised in large families in rural communities. Dad's father was an immigrant from England and Mother's was the son of earlier settlers. They combined the heritages of this land and others in the melting pot of America, growing up with an abundance of siblings, few material goods, lots of love, and a healthy respect for hard work and self-sufficiency. In both families it was expected that young people would graduate from high school and then go to work. College was not considered, being too expensive and unfamiliar. After high school, then, Mother got a job in a department store selling domestics and Dad worked in a small furniture store.

In the spring of 1936 my parents met at the Shadow Lake Dance Hall—a gathering place for the local young people. Dad arrived with a group of buddies from his high school and Mother came with school chums from hers. They met, danced, drove home in his navy blue roadster and began "seeing each other."

After a courtship of almost four years, they became engaged and started to plan their future. Theirs was the American dream of the early forties: to buy some land, to build a home, to have a small family, and to give their children some of the opportunities they never had.

And then, on a chilly December 7 in 1941, events took their plans and threw them to the wind. Dad joined the Navy and was gone. Mother was left with an engagement ring and a promise. The war in the Pacific was a whirlwind, and daily reports of casualties filled the papers. The scanty V-Mail brought little encouragement—terse, uninformative lines and stilted "I-love-you"'s wedged between official remonstrations to remember the need for security and censorship.

Mother, in her spare time, volunteered at the USO, wrote to her absent fiancé daily, scoured the papers and radio news for any details of his whereabouts, and prayed for his safety.

For three long years Dad rode a supply ship in the South Pacific and Mother waited at home, saving her money, collecting things for her hope chest, daily writing her letters.

Then, one day in September of 1944, Dad showed up on his fiancée's doorstep. He was reassigned to a duty station in New York to teach Navy storekeeping. This time when he left, she followed by train, and on a snowy November afternoon they were married in Geneva, New York. After the ceremony they took a bus to Niagra Falls for their honeymoon.

When the war finally ended, they returned to their hometown, bought a piece of property, anticipated the birth of their first child, and planned their first home. Their nest egg was tiny, but so was their house—850 square feet, most of which they finished and painted themselves.

Slowly, carefully, they saved their money, making wise investments when time and opportunities were right. The family was always together for breakfast and dinner, and the conversations were laced with laughter, dreams, and funny stories gleaned from my father's business. We were a family based on the firm foundation of the love and respect my parents had for each other. Their relationship was the basis for all we had and did.

Perhaps their love story is not unusual for couples of their day and age; I see it as a thing of rare beauty. It is a valentine cut from the fabric of American life, reflecting a period of time we may never see again. It is a testimony to the power of mutual respect, self-sacrifice, and dedication. And on Valentine's Day it is important to be reminded that that kind of love still exists.

Painting Overleaf
WINTER HOME
The Photo Source

Valentine Box

Inez Baker

After Christmas, winter weather
Dominated every scene;
Days grew shorter, no vacations
Interrupted school routine.

Then a new excitement beckoned,
Gave us children things to do,
Let us handle colored papers,
Work with scissors and with glue.

First we cut the bright crepe paper
In strips marked by penciled lines,
Then 'twas pasted on a carton
That would hold our valentines.

When the box was finished, perfect,
In its glory it would stand
While again we children labored
Making valentines by hand.

Labeled with the names of classmates,
Hearts of paper decked with lace,
Slipped into the slotted boxtop,
Filled the box at rapid pace.

Anticipation bubbled over
Til, at last, the Big Day came;
Each child shared the box's contents
As the teacher called each name.

When that day we all trudged homeward
With our pretty valentines,
We knew winter's end was closer,
Spring could not be far behind.

Keepsakes

Edna Jaques

A pressed rose from a bride's bouquet
    That someone loved and tucked away
Between the pages of a book;
    A blurred old snap that someone took
That caught, as in a fleeting glance,
    One precious moment of romance.

A stoppered bottle of perfume
    Given a bridesmaid by a groom
Who has been gone these forty years;
    A hankie never meant for tears,
A square of Irish lace and lawn
    With tiny stitched initials on.

An old book of the British Isles,
    A lady's magazine with styles
Of half a century ago;
    A Christmas card of drifted snow
Showing a church with open doors,
    From which the golden lamplight pours.

A keepsake precious as a gem
    Reminding her of each of them.

Photo Opposite
TOKENS OF YESTERYEAR
H. Armstrong Roberts, Inc.

My Heart Is Like an Attic

June Masters Bacher

My heart is like an attic:
It has so much in store
That every rafter's sagging
And it can hold no more.

I wonder why it gathered
So much from yesterday
Which now, outgrown and useless,
Will not be thrown away?

It needs to hold an auction
Of what it can't revive;
But memories-dim, when threatened,
Come suddenly alive

As if they know a secret
That even I don't share:
They know my heart is foolish
And it will leave them there.

Old souvenirs and trinkets. . .
A flower curled and brown
Saved when the hometown victors
All tore the goalpost down. . .

I guess they'll always stay there,
Those sentimental things
That make my heart an attic
And give it silent wings.

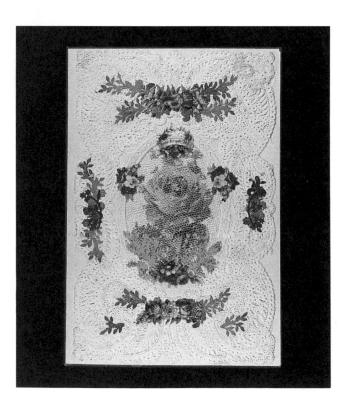

The sweetness and sentiment which Americans pass on to one another through valentines is a centuries-old tradition. In addition to what we see on card racks in stores, there is a whole world of valentines collected from years past.

Because valentines convey the feelings of one person for another, people tend to tuck their old valentines into dark dresser drawers, old shoe boxes, or attic chests to sit and age with other mementos of times past and love shared. There also exist collectors who buy old valentines as investments. And if you collect valentines, whether for sentimental reasons or otherwise, you probably know there is a rich history which feeds this important tradition.

Most collectible valentines date from the 1800s to the 1930s, but the history of valentines dates back to Rome in 270 A.D. There, according to legend, a young priest named Valentinus was sentenced to execution by Emperor Claudius II for refusing to renounce Christian teachings. While in jail, he helped restore the sight of the jailkeeper's young daughter, who had been going blind. On the day of his execution, February 14, he plucked a heart-shaped leaf from a clump of violets outside his jail window and pierced it with a note for her on which he had written, "From your Valentine."

The legend of St. Valentine filtered down through the centuries in France, Scotland, Wales, and Germany, reaching the United States about 150 years ago. The charm of the Valentine's Day remembrance, however, came into full flower during England's elegant Regency period (early 1800s), between the time of the quill pen and Spencerian script, and continued into the industrial/manufacturing age.

Valentine's Day has always been associated with expressions of love, and a whole language of flowers exists which explains the type and depth of love expressed through a valentine. Forget-me-nots represent faithfulness and longevity and pansies, thoughtfulness. Roses represent several kinds of love; pink indicates friendship; one red rose represents romantic love; white indicates purity, as for a bride. Lilies of the valley also represent purity; and in Victorian times, a valentine from a young woman to a man with a white rose or lily of the valley on it indicated she was ready for marriage. From man to woman, the same white rose or lily was considered a proposal of marriage in February to be followed by a June wedding.

Queen Victoria of England, who enjoyed a long and popular reign (1837-1901), indirectly began a new tradition in valentines. A folk heroine to her subjects, her image was often pictured on valentines of that period. Later in the United States, the images of Jenny Lind, Lillian Russell, and other actresses were found on cards. The list of names even grew to include such folk heros of the screen as Snow White, Mickey Mouse, and Popeye!

Among the valentines most sought after by collectors are sailor valentines; fracture work (cut or pricked paper); and elaborate, large-scale representations of ships, planes, and trains. The sailor valentines began to appear in the 1880s in North America from seamen who, away from home for months at a time, would collect seashells to make into valentines for their sweethearts. These were often octagonal, double-sided, hinged boxes which opened to reveal a message fashioned in lines of tiny seashells, such as "Love the giver."

In early nineteenth-century America, the charm of Valentine's Day inspired the Pennsylvania Dutch to cut lovely cards using newspaper and construction paper. In Virginia, silhouettes originated that were hand-scissored with incredible care.

Pinprick lace designs and dried flower cages which opened to reveal a tender sentiment also were popular. For many, the art of assembling one's paper fancy meant diligently building up three-dimensional tiers of lacy papers, tiny flowers, and beads on silk or satin, then penning a "Will you be mine?" sentiment. Many of these fracture-work paper designs employ hundreds of individual cuts or pinpricks to achieve the overall design.

What is the most enduring quality of a valentine? The quality of giving from one person to another. From making or purchasing that perfect valentine for another person to enjoying collecting valentines from the past, we each have the opportunity to continue the valentine tradition. And the history and variety of cards, including those available to us in stores today, tell us through sheer numbers that there are a million wonderful ways to say, "I love you."

Valentines from the collection of Evalene Pulati

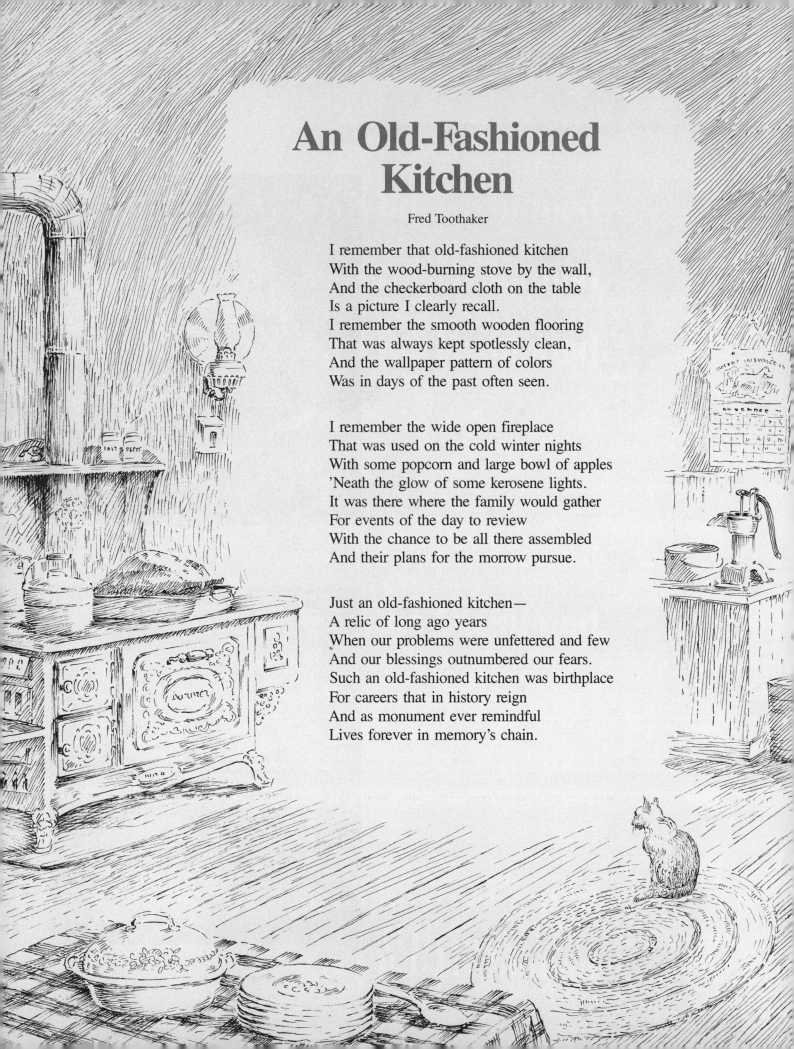

An Old-Fashioned Kitchen

Fred Toothaker

I remember that old-fashioned kitchen
With the wood-burning stove by the wall,
And the checkerboard cloth on the table
Is a picture I clearly recall.
I remember the smooth wooden flooring
That was always kept spotlessly clean,
And the wallpaper pattern of colors
Was in days of the past often seen.

I remember the wide open fireplace
That was used on the cold winter nights
With some popcorn and large bowl of apples
'Neath the glow of some kerosene lights.
It was there where the family would gather
For events of the day to review
With the chance to be all there assembled
And their plans for the morrow pursue.

Just an old-fashioned kitchen—
A relic of long ago years
When our problems were unfettered and few
And our blessings outnumbered our fears.
Such an old-fashioned kitchen was birthplace
For careers that in history reign
And as monument ever remindful
Lives forever in memory's chain.

Links with the Past

Edna Jaques

Maybe it's only an old cracked plate
Or a saucer with roses on,
A picture hanging upon the wall
Of a window with curtains drawn,
The scent of mint from a wooded slope
Or a primrose with fluted skirts,
And sometimes the sound of a favorite hymn—
All are pleasures that almost hurt.

The faded blue of an old man's eyes,
Or a timid shuffling step,
Can tap the spring in your spirit's depth
Where the tears of a heart are kept.
The spangled meadows of early May
Can make you a child again,
Gathering flowers for golden hearts
To weave in a daisy chain.

Apricot jam in a crystal jar
Or a dogwood tree in bloom
Can bring on the past like a colored slide
Shown in a darkened room.
As time goes by and the years unfold,
How precious the old days seem—
A home you loved and a hand you touched,
And a lantern's cheerful gleam.

Links with the past, how they bless and burn,
Yet are rich in remembered grace:
A quiet street and an open gate,
And the smile on a dear one's face.

We Need No Words, Dear

Grace E. Easley

We need no words to ever say
The thoughts we share alone;
Our little smiles, our little sighs
Speak volumes of their own!
We need no words to understand
The happiness we know;
One gentle look so deeply felt,
Is all that needs to show!

We need no words to emphasize
The closeness that we feel;
Our two hands locked together
Is proof enough it's real.
We need no words to say the things
Most people long to hear,
For in our hearts there glows a warmth
Whenever we are near!

There comes a dear awareness
As our eyes light up to see
Each other's face . . . now tell me,
What need for words have we?
The years have made us mellow
And the trials have made us strong;
And as long as we're together,
Nothing else can matter long!

No words of any language,
However sweet and fair,
Can say so well "I love you"
As your lips upon my hair!
And no phrase ever written
Can ever match the tone
Of my arms about you only
And my cheek against your own!

Photo Opposite
WINTER WALK
H. Armstrong Roberts, Inc.

True Love

Phyllis C. Michael

I've often heard it said that love
   Is such a fragile thing,
A whim snuffed out by wind and wave,
   Mere thistledown on wing.

But you and I both know, my dear,
   This notion is all wrong:
True love can never, never die,
   It's one unending song.

Oh, yes! There may come minor chords,
   A storm or two or three,
But love, true love like yours and mine
   Will live eternally.

For love is not a gown to wear
    When comes a sunny day;
It's like a fine, all-weather coat
    You choose for come-what-may.

Love shelters you from desert heat
    And from each needless care;
It keeps you safe from winter chill,
    Unseen—it's always there.

True love is made in heaven above,
    And God and you and I
Will prove to all the doubting world
    True love can never die.

Living Valentine

Craig E. Sathoff

The valentine you gave to me,
All frills and fancy lace,
Makes happiness bloom in my heart,
A smile light up my face.

For valentines are like bouquets,
They have a special way
Of adding bits of loveliness
To beautify the day.

I treasure this one valentine,
For it has come to say
What in your every word and deed
You prove to me each day.

In giving me your love and trust,
In everything you do,
You are my living valentine
To last a lifetime through.

SWEET SENTIMENTS
Envision

The Greatest of

Norma Nolan Santangelo

Peace
is a dove with folded wings,
nesting in the heart that sings;

Truth
is a burning flame of blue—
steady, unflinching, piercing through;

Kindness
is like a violet shy,
doing good where none espy;

Patience
is an endless tide
with hope and faith secure inside;

Strength
is like a sturdy oak,
stalwart, upright, supporting folk;

These Is Love

Hope
is like a butterfly,
flitting, flirting—low, then high;

Faith
is like the ocean deep,
heavy, silent, yet never asleep;

Compassion
like soft arms of prayer—
protecting, enveloping in its care;

Joy
is a brook that bubbles along
and fills the air with a glad song;

And Love
is like a full-blown rose,
the morning star and the sunset's close,
life's rich wine to young and old,
an angel's crown of purest gold!

I'll Gather Stardust

Clay Harrison

I'll gather stardust to make you a crown;
I'll gather rainbows to make you a gown.
I'll pick the first roses blooming in spring
And have them delivered by angels on wing.

I'll fashion a ring of pure autumn gold
To be yours forever to have and to hold.
I'll string all the pearls found deep in the sea
And wrap them with moonlight to shine endlessly.

I'll tell the songbirds to sing you a song
Whenever you're lonely and nights are too long.
I'll give you my heart, my soul, and my life
If you will accept them and be my wife.

Photo Opposite
LOVE IN BLOOM
Robert Barclay
Grant Heilman Photography

Young Love

Joy Belle Burgess

Love is the glow of something—
So holy and divine—
It reaches out to touch young hearts
With happiness sublime.

Love is something beautiful
Reflected in their sighs—
The radiant glow and sparkling star
Of love light in their eyes.

Love is the breath of springtime—
The sweetest thing on earth—
That breezes into waiting hearts
To fill their days with mirth.

Love makes their toes trip lightly
As they dance their way along,
As two in love find happiness
Then soar on wings of song.

Enduring Love

Virginia Peace

My love for you grows deeper
As each year passes by;
I sometimes sit and contemplate
Upon the reasons why.

I love you for your gentleness
In things you do and say,
And for the thoughtfulness you show
A hundred times a day.

I love you for your courage
And your wisdom when you speak;
They give to me the inner strength
I need when I am weak.

Some grow old regretfully
But I will age with pride;
I'll keep my love forever true
And walk close by your side.

The Glory of the Rose

Joanne Kash
Cherie Gardner

Editor's Note for "The Glory of the Rose"

Cherie Gardner, an accomplished writer and gardener for many of her eighty-one years, has long been a champion of the rose. Due in part to her efforts, the Honorable Bill Chappell, Jr., representative from Florida, cosponsored a joint resolution in the U.S. Congress to designate the rose as our national flower. On October 7, 1986, President Ronald Reagan signed the bill into law. Rep. Chappell submitted for the Congressional Record *Ms. Gardner's essay "The Glory of the Rose" on October 16, 1986. (A condensed version of the essay follows.)*

The rose has been known and celebrated since the earliest hours of history. Mentioned often in story and song, it is the eternal flower, an everlasting emblem of sentiment, a flower for all classes of people.

The rose grows wild in temperate zones throughout the world. When the American pioneers poured over the Allegheny Mountains and into the plains of Kentucky and Ohio, and later onto the prairies of the West, they found the wild rose growing everywhere. Many prairie homes were enriched by the splendor and color of wild roses, bringing peace and sentiment in hours of loneliness and struggle, and brightening many a frontier wedding.

The fables of antiquity feature the rose. It was identified with Cupid and Venus (called Eros and Aphrodite, respectively) by the Greeks. They considered the rose the symbol of joy and love and, at the same time, of prudence.

The Romans placed a rose over the door during a feast, and whoever passed under it recognized a solemn obligation not to reveal what was seen or heard. From this custom came the term "sub rosa," meaning "under the rose," applied to anything done in confidence. Later the rose was placed at the entrance to confessionals in Rome as a symbol of secrecy.

During the days of feudalism and chivalry, the rose was the accepted "badge of favor." Sturdy knights and mighty warriors battled with one another to win the rose of some fair lady.

During the Renaissance, when Dante thought of the beauty of queenly Beatrice, he sang sonnets about the rose. But to trace the impact the rose has left on literature would be to compile the work of all authors and poets. Never has a man or woman achieved fame in letters without writing about the rose. The literature of Europe and America is replete with it.

In poetry, the rose always has symbolized purity and innocence. Anacreon, the great lyric poet of the sixth century B.C., wrote of the origin of the rose, which he claimed sprang from Venus' blushes when she was bathing and caught Jupiter spying on her. Shakespeare mentions the rose at least seventy times. His Juliet asks, "What's in a name? That which we call a rose by any other name would smell as sweet."

In art, as in literature, the presence of the rose goes back to the very dawn of civilization. Greek, Roman, Egyptian, and Assyrian artists all employed it in their work. And the Etruscan rose is almost as famous as the Etruscan vase.

As the centuries progressed, roses became common in family gardens. And the uses to which they were put brought a fuller realization of the glory and beauty of the rose to every nature lover. The rush of commercialism in the early days of the industrial age, however, seemed to sweep away all sentiment, all love for the leisurely joy of growing things. Then, with the advent of greater prosperity after the turn of the century, America expressed again that old desire, that old longing for a "vine over the door."

In today's cities, even modest gardens outrank those of the aristocracy of the past. Many homes include larger and more beautiful gardens than those of colonial America. Often modern gardeners barely break the sod before their thoughts turn to the beauty of roses blooming in the spring.

The rose is perennial, unlike annuals which endure for a season, but must be replanted each spring. The rose blooms the first season and continues to repay the gardener with fragrance and flowers throughout the years. As long as there are people to give, receive, and admire roses, the appeal of their fragrance and form will endure.

Photo Opposite
GLORY OF THE ROSE
Al Riccio
H. Armstrong Roberts, Inc.

Life's Beautiful Years

Phyllis C. Michael

Oh, the years of our lives are as a day
When we live with someone we love,
When we walk hand in hand through joy or pain
Looking to God above.

Those beautiful years are but as one step
Along the happiness road
When we've shared by faith each new day's cares,
Each portion of life's checkered load.

Those wonderful years are like a true pearl
Slowly shaped to last,
Aglow with the warmth of each sacrifice,
Each memory of the past.

They're jeweled in trust, more precious than silver,
More precious even than gold,
Sent each day from God's storehouse of life
For us to have and to hold.

Those wonderful years are but as Act One
Of a play in which love conquers fear;
Dear God, grant that we may live hand in hand
Through bountiful, beautiful years.

Heart Sachets and Heart Garland

Ann Marie Braaten

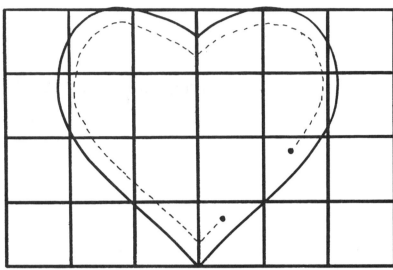

one square equals one inch

Step 1

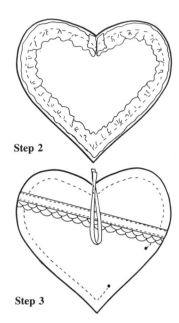

Step 2

Step 3

Sachet Supplies

(makes 5 sachets)

⅛ yard fabric

assorted laces and ribbons:

    ⅛ yard of ⅛″ ribbon for one loop (used for hanging sachet)

    ⅜ yard gathered lace for edging one heart

    ⅛ yard lace or ribbon for any design (horizontal, vertical or diagonal)

    ¼ yard of ⅛″ ribbon for one bow

small silk flowers

polyester batting sprinkled with a favorite scent or potpourri

matching thread

Garland Supplies

⅛ yard fabric

1¼ yard of ⅛″ satin lace

2 yards of ⅜″ satin ribbon

10 small silk flowers

polyester batting or potpourri

matching thread

2½″ plastic rings (optional)

Sachet Directions

Step One: Cutting

Using the heart pattern, cut two fabric hearts for each sachet.

Step Two: Designing the Sachet Front

1. For sachet with gathered lace edging the heart shape, place lace right side down on the right side of fabric. Sew lace to heart, leaving a ¼-inch seam allowance.
2. For sachet with horizontal, vertical, or diagonal lace and ribbon, sew the trims right side up to the right side of fabric heart.

Step Three: Attaching Loop

Hand baste ⅛″ wide satin ribbon loop on the seam line of heart front.

Step Four: Sewing Front to Back

1. With right sides together, pin and sew heart back to heart front leaving a 1½-inch opening on the seamline.

2. Clip curves.
3. Turn heart to right side through opening.
4. Fill sachet with scented batting or potpourri.
5. Hand sew opening closed.

Step Five: Adding Silk Flowers

1. Tie a bow around the small silk flowers.
2. Hand sew flowers to sachet.

Garland Directions

Follow steps one, four, and five for sachets.

Step Six: Finishing Garland

1. Hand sew the five hearts together at a point in the side seam.
2. Hand sew a bow (each made with one yard of ⅜-inch satin ribbon) on each end of the garland.
3. (Optional) Hand sew one plastic ring on the back of each of the end hearts. These can be used to hang the garland on a wall.

Photo Opposite
VALENTINE SACHETS
Nancy Robinson

Sawdust and Dreams

Edgar A. Guest

One time a little girl came to me crying because her doll had gotten caught on a nail and where the cambric was torn, the doll's insides had come pouring out, and the child discovered them to be—only sawdust. Someone—some cynical grown-up who hadn't anything better to do than destroy a child's illusions—had chided her with the fact that the doll she had loved so passionately was only a thing of wax and sawdust after all. So she came to me crying bitterly. I gathered her up in my arms and after promising to have the doll mended so as to hold the sawdust in, and have her face cleaned up and made as good—or almost as good—as new, I tried to explain to her that her doll, while she loved it and cared for it, was something more than sawdust and wax. Her love for it and dreams about it made it something more, clothed it with the beautiful stuff of fairy tale and illusion. When she had gone away, pacified and content, I thought to myself, "There are too many people in this world who try to reason in terms of cold realities only, who don't take account of the dreams which change harsh realities, if only we'll let them."

"Ah," the scoffing cynic said,
"You thought your doll a lovely thing.
You took it in your arms in bed
And fancied it worth cherishing.
But now it's broken, child, and you
Shed tears above it in despair.
This is a foolish thing you do.
There's merely wax and sawdust there."

Said one unto the weeping child
Who knew the truth as well as he:
"Come, little one, be reconciled!
Perhaps your doll can mended be.
Forget the sawdust you have seen.
Forget this grim and dreadful truth.
Such tragedies as this have been
An everlasting part of youth.

"So keep your love of dolls, my dear,
And cherish them the while you may.
You'll find with every passing year
That many a joy must go away.
Cling fast to beauty though it fades
And press your playthings to your heart.
When reason cold your mind invades,
Then much that's tender must depart.

"So treasure wax and sawdust things
Which warm the soul and glad the eye.
Heed not the cynic's mutterings
Who coldly reasons how and why.
'Tis well to love the good and true,
But keep your dreams and fancies here
And never grow so wise that you
Are left with naught to do but sneer."

Photo Overleaf
WINTER BALLOON FESTIVAL
MADISON, WISCONSIN
Ken Dequaine

Skaters at Night

Vera Laurel Hoffman

Our breath is frosty on the air,
Our footsteps echo everywhere;
Across the frozen white snow scene
Once more our earth looks fresh and clean.
A red sled waits beside the door,
And skates are ready to explore
The silver sheen of ponds that glow
Like diamonds on the sparkling snow.

Bonfires warm the winter night
With little spots of flaming light;
Gay voices—laughter sounding clear—
Are bell-like in the atmosphere.
While flashing by on wings of steel
With bright scarves flying that reveal
The rainbow colors green, blue, red,
Warm caps hug the skaters' heads.

The night holds magic, soft and clear,
The whirling sounds of winds are here;
Each snowflake star that settles down
In minute beauty all around—
Blending with others where we stand—
Has made our world a wonderland!

JAY KILLIAN

Coasting

Leona Bolt Martin

We used to climb the highest hill
The little city boasted
And pull resisting sleds behind. . .
Then *down* the hill we coasted.

The metal runners cut deep grooves
In the snowy, icebound road,
And it required a steady hand
To steer that heavy load.

The "tailman" always ran and pushed
To help us get well-started;
The weighted bobsleds skimmed the ground
With shrieks from the fainthearted!

Now many snows have come and gone,
Our lives have moved apart;
But memories of youthful days
Are treasured in each heart.

Photo Opposite
UP THE HILL
H. Armstrong Roberts, Inc.

The Oldest Valentine

Marvin Jordon

On the edge of a little country town
Stands a large and ageless oak.
Defying storms and Father Time,
It's a living shrine to folk.

Supporting many broken limbs,
The trunk in spots is bare.
But the hand-carved heart and arrow,
With hand-carved initials, is there.

A day for valentines each year
Brings opportunity.
The paper hearts won't last as long
As the one on that ageless tree.

Childhood Valentine

Dan A. Hoover

Happy days of hearts and flowers,
When even seconds seemed like hours,
As the one I would be mine
Took my homemade valentine,
Read my scrawl with big, blue eyes,
And smiled with innocent surprise.

Dear, sweet days when hearts were young,
Music and laughter mixed among
Knickerbockers, pinafores,
School books carried to little girls' doors.
Golden arrows, tender hearts:
Memories of childhood sweethearts.

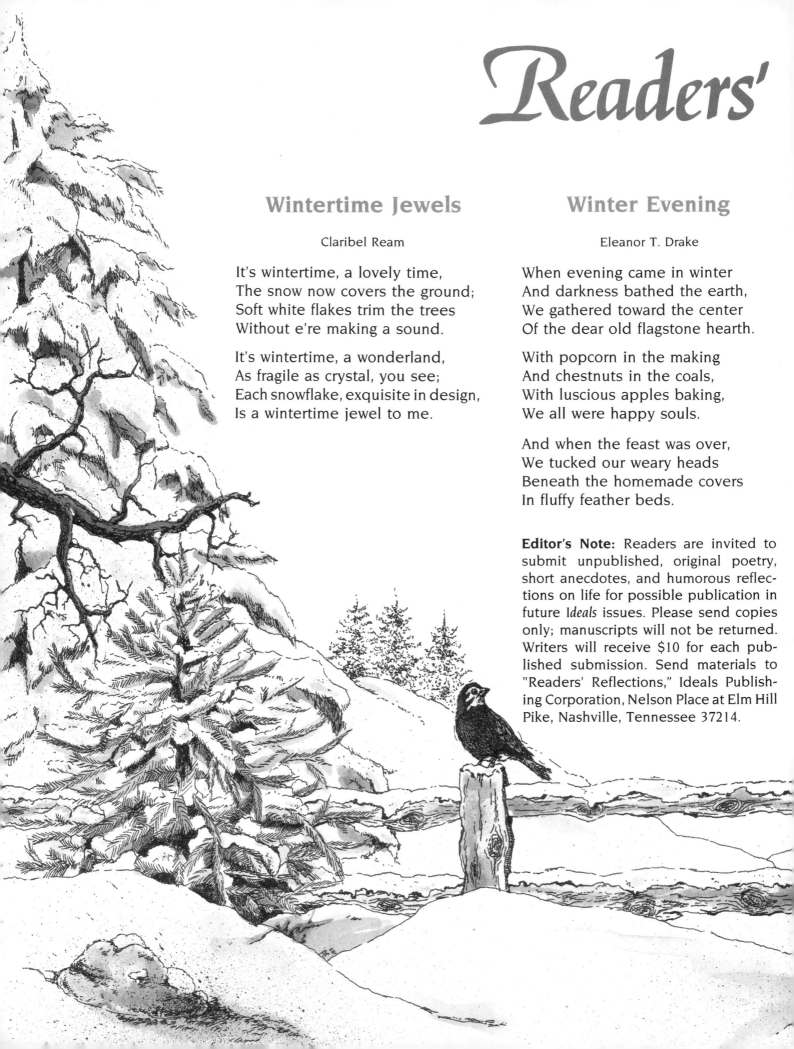

Readers'

Wintertime Jewels

Claribel Ream

It's wintertime, a lovely time,
The snow now covers the ground;
Soft white flakes trim the trees
Without e're making a sound.

It's wintertime, a wonderland,
As fragile as crystal, you see;
Each snowflake, exquisite in design,
Is a wintertime jewel to me.

Winter Evening

Eleanor T. Drake

When evening came in winter
And darkness bathed the earth,
We gathered toward the center
Of the dear old flagstone hearth.

With popcorn in the making
And chestnuts in the coals,
With luscious apples baking,
We all were happy souls.

And when the feast was over,
We tucked our weary heads
Beneath the homemade covers
In fluffy feather beds.

Editor's Note: Readers are invited to submit unpublished, original poetry, short anecdotes, and humorous reflections on life for possible publication in future I*deals* issues. Please send copies only; manuscripts will not be returned. Writers will receive $10 for each published submission. Send materials to "Readers' Reflections," Ideals Publishing Corporation, Nelson Place at Elm Hill Pike, Nashville, Tennessee 37214.

Reflections

Significant Snow

Ron Evans

Have you ever walked in significant
   snow—
Not just a skiff, but after a blow—
When it strains the sapling spruce
   tree's limb
And makes the stiff-necked laurel
   bend?

You can ignore all aggravation,
Indulge in sweet procrastination,
Express such grand exhilaration
With the morning's piled
   accumulation;

Then evening sun casts a golden glow
Over crests of gently drifted snow
And we're humbled by the quiet
As the light begins to die.

We sense the forest change its
   mood—
So silent, even thoughts intrude—
And for an instant understand
We've seen God's face and touched
   his hand.

Communion

June C. Bush

I watched the snowflakes falling,
Softly, gently, all around,
And piling ever higher
Without making any sound.

I felt your nearness, dearness,
While our hearts in rhythm beat—
Our thoughts and feelings mingling
In communion ever sweet.

Like snowflakes falling endlessly
And settling to the ground,
We felt our love grow deeper
Without making any sound.

God Had Bid You Meet

Garnett Ann Schultz

Someone may cross your path today
 You've never met before,
Someone you'll love and understand,
 A friend forevermore.
With eager heart and happy thought
 You'll find a treasure sweet,
And you shall know without a doubt
 That God had bid you meet.

Someone may touch your life today
 For just a little while
(Perhaps in one bright, tender glance,
 One warm and friendly smile)
To never come your way again,
 And yet that moment sweet
Could add a charm you won't forget
 Though not again you'll meet.

Someone may shake your outstretched hand
 In warmth and glowing pride;
'Tis then you'll feel a sunbeam there,
 A happiness inside.
And though it be just one brief hour
 You'll know a love complete;
Acquaintance—or a lasting friend—
 'Tis God that meant you'd meet.

My Friend

Craig E. Sathoff

The value of a trusting friend
   I never really knew
Until one lucky day I chanced
   To find a friend like you.

It seems to guide my every step
   And every deed I do
To know that I've a loyal friend
   To tell my wishes to.

For friendship brings a state of mind
   That manifests a peace,
A warming glow of happiness,
   A meaningful release.

If friendship strengthens as it grows,
   The years that are to be
Shall be especially blessed, friend,
   With joys for you and me.

Winter's Dream

R.C. Stanley

Filmy fingers of hoary mist
Cross craggy peaks and curl and twist,
Rising above new-fallen snow,
Cool and clean in its mystic glow.

Sentinel trees in wintry garb
Stand disguised as icy barbs,
While in the valley dark and deep
Lonely winds moan and weep
Fragile tears of ancient frost;
And all life forms seem crystal lost.

Yet proud rebel peaks seem to rise
In freedom reaching for the skies
Which promise in a veil of blue
That winter's days are growing few.

With this glad promise of new life,
Shadows close on winter's night;
And slowly dies the mystic glow
Of cool and clean new-fallen snow
Where tired fingers curl and twist
'Round craggy peaks lost in mist.

Photo Opposite
GREAT FALLS
PATERSON, NEW JERSEY
Gene Ahrens

Contentment

Vera Hardman

A winter's day—a glowing fire—
A slender book of verse
Bring wealth to rival Midas
No matter what your purse.

To far lands you may travel
With a good book at your side,
Sharing life with others,
New doors opening wide.

The glowing fire—the book of verse—
Adventure time to treasure,
Glad moments that will light your life
With contented pleasure.

Winter Evening

Carol Bessent Hayman

The snow has fallen like a winter blanket,
Fleecy and light like soft white cotton.
We light the fire inside our room for living
And think of old scenes, friends too long forgotten.

We watch the twilight cast its dark reflections
Over bright snowfall.
Winter evenings are made for quiet love
And recollections.

Photo Overleaf
SKATERS AT DUSK
MADISON, WISCONSIN
Ken Dequaine

Winter Wood

Grace E. Easley

I grew up with this forest, and I knew
These giant trees when they were nothing more

Than slender saplings swaying in the breeze. . .
Sought solitude, delighted in the lore

Of nature who became my teacher first. . .
Walked down trails where sun and shadows meet,

In silence softly tucked about the days. . .
Traced the twists and turns of every creek. . .

Stepped lightly through the days' after-glow,
Amid the falling flakes of silver white,

Belonging to the moment and the mood,
Another little creature of the night,

With quickened breath and ears attuned, who stood
Sensing God within this winter wood.

Winter Walk

Earle J. Grant

Down a country road we go,
Amid a landscape embossed with snow,

Slender poplars edge the way,
Lovely in silver overlay,

Weathered fence posts are stitched in
 white,
And fat cattle amble into sight,

A rabbit hops down a velvet field
Looking for food, but he finds no yield,

Smoke plumes ascend from each
 homestead
Against a sky that has turned to lead.

A lake down the valley glistens with ice,
A picture-book view that has no price . . .

This winter walk is a time to treasure
Presenting God's beauty without measure!

It's Always April in My Heart

Clay Harrison

It's always April in my heart,
Even when birds and leaves depart,
The winds may bring their chill embrace,
But there's a smile upon my face
Recalling roses on the vine
And memories as warm as wine.

Sensing tulips and daffodils,
I rest with snow upon the hills;
Coming soon are lilies, too,
And in my heart the sky is blue.
Then just when all the clouds seem gray,
I pull out rainbows tucked away.

So let the seasons stop and start;
It's always April in my heart!

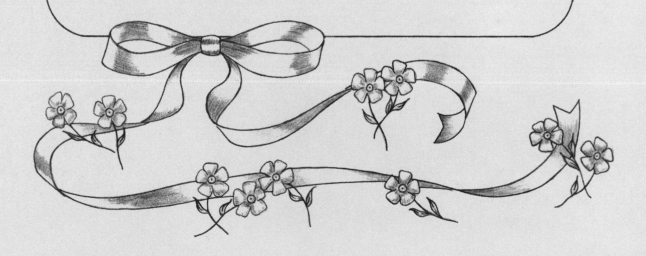

Photo Opposite
WINTER BLOOMS
Jack Zehrt

Country Chronicle

Lansing Christman

Lucile walks with me today to the winter woods still heavy with snow. The days are lengthening. It is February, and we know there will be early signs of winter waning. As we walk, we anticipate changes in the woods and swamps, the creek banks, and warm pasture springs.

Here on this Valentine's Day, we see swollen buds on maple and basswood trees, on ash and oak. The soothing gray-blue sky reminds us of spring. A new softness replaces the dull, cheerless brown of fall and the somber of mid-winter.

As we walk among the trees, the rays of the sun sprinkle glistening jewels of light on the ground ahead of our footsteps. There is artistry here to match the lace-like work on an old-time valentine I remember stored in an album somewhere, perhaps in an attic chest, where etched against a background of white are intricate shadows of tree trunks, branches and twigs. Their images are much like the delicate designs of frost on a windowpane.

In the swamps and along the sluggish stream, we see that osiers have turned a fiery red. Pussy willow catkins and those of the alders have swollen where they border the channels of the stream. There muskrats swim under a shield of thin ice. Around a spring on the pasture slope, facing the south, the grass seems as fresh and green as after an April rain.

In the old apple orchard on the knoll, we sense that March blossoms are already underway. Listen! There's the rich liquid warble of the first bluebird! And there's a robin's carol from the maples by the road. We listen long to these welcome warblers. Their songs are our serenade to enduring life and love.

Not Long Now

Helen Harrington

What if the heavy north winds sigh
And clouds are gray across the sky
And snow surrounds both you and me,
Covering every building and tree?

Be cheerful still, for there are rays
Of sunshine now among the days;
And often in the briefer nights
The wind dies down, the moon is bright.

Now and then, within my heart
I feel a joyous trembling start;
And then I let my spirit sing
To celebrate the coming spring!

Photo Opposite
FIRST DAFFODIL
Don Eastman
The Stock Solution

Promise

Diane Griffith

Today amidst the melting snow
And winter's dwindling wrath,
I saw a purple violet
Along my garden path.

What makes this fragile flower grow,
New life upon a stem?
More precious than an amethyst,
It's nature's special gem!

As I gently brush the snow away,
I hear my own heart sing,
For here on a fading winter day
Is born the promise of spring!

March

Gustaf W. Von Colln

The song sparrow sings atop the spruce
With brilliant melodies profuse;
The frost is melting in the ground
And harbor ice is outward bound.

The snow's reduced to tiny patches,
And heaven's blue goes by in snatches.
A sudden rain with wind's increase
Causes all birdsong to cease.

Signs are here of winter's end
And of a friendlier, gentler trend.
Thank God for trials safely borne
And hope of spring some early morn.

Celebrate the Renewal of Life
with *Easter* Ideals

• Admire a breathtaking tree in full spring bloom,

• Watch the excitement of discovery of the joys of Easter on the face of a child,

• Celebrate the glory of our Lord riding into Jerusalem in triumph,

• Marvel at Russian-decorated Easter eggs—exotic, intricate, elegant.

All these and more are in our next issue, *Easter Ideals.* The magnificent photography paired with inspirational poetry and informative articles, the popular "Readers' Reflections," and a recipe or two provide a feast for the eye and heart.

With each issue, *Ideals* strives toward excellence in a wholesome, uplifting publication. Doris K. Nelson, who lives in San Mateo, California, writes:

> *I would like to express my delight in reading each new issue. The beautiful thoughts, poems, and pictures are exceptional and spiritually uplifting. I have given several gifts of* Ideals *subscriptions to friends and family, and they all treasure the gift. Keep your beautiful magazine with its high ideals!*

Thank you Doris Nelson! Wouldn't spring be the perfect time to share *Ideals* with a friend? Start a subscription today—with *Easter Ideals.*

ACKNOWLEDGMENTS

SAWDUST AND DREAMS from *EDGAR A. GUEST BROADCASTING,* copyright 1935, The Reilly & Lee Co. Used by permission; FEBRUARY by Edna Jaques from *THE GOLDEN ROAD,* copyright 1953 by Thomas Allen & Son Limited, Markham, Ontario, Canada; KEEPSAKES by Edna Jaques from *THE GOLDEN ROAD,* copyright 1953 by Thomas Allen & Son Limited, Markham, Ontario, Canada. Our sincere thanks to the following whose addresses we were unable to locate: Elsie Natalie Brady for FLOWERS IN WINTER; Grace E. Easley for WE NEED NO WORDS, DEAR and WINTER WOOD; Diane Griffith for PROMISE; Leona Bolt Martin for COASTING; Virginia Peace for ENDURING LOVE; B.C. Stanley for WINTER'S DREAM; Fred Toothaker for AN OLD-FASHIONED KITCHEN; Stella Craft Tremble for TOGETHER from *HAPPY HOLIDAYS.* VOL. 2, copyright 1974 by the author; Gustaf W. Von Colln for MARCH.

Statement of ownership, management, and circulation (Required by 39 U.S.C. 3685), of IDEALS, published 8 times a year in February, March, May, June, August, September, November, and December at Nashville, Tennessee, for September 1987. Publisher, Patricia A. Pingry; Editor, Peggy Schaefer; Managing Editor, as above; Owner, Egmont U.S., Inc., wholly owned subsidiary of The Egmont H. Petersen Foundation, VOGNMAGER-GADE 11, 1148 Copenhagen, K, Denmark. The known bondholders, mortgages, and other security holders owning or holding 1 percent or more of total amount of bonds, mortgages, or other securities are: None. Average no. copies each issue during preceding 12 months: Total no. copies printed (Net Press Run) 235,261. Paid circulation 51,071. Mail subscription 177,479. Total paid circulation 228,550. Free distribution 654. Total distribution 229,204. Actual no. copies of single issue published nearest to filing date: Total no. copies printed (Net Press Run) 177,083. Paid circulation 7,940. Mail subscription 162,223. Total paid circulation 170,163. Free distribution 465. Total distribution 170,628. I certify that the statements made by me above are correct and complete. Patricia A. Pingry, Publisher.